Boundaries In Dating

Set Boundaries Find Love

Knowing When To Draw The Lines And When To Take The Leap Forward

Marilyn Cook

Table of Contents

Chapter 1: **10 signs You're In A Healthy Relationship** 5

Chapter 2: *8 Signs You Were Actually In Love* 12

Chapter 3: *6 Ways To Flirt With Someone* 15

Chapter 4: 6 Ways To Deal With Rude People 19

Chapter 5: 9 Tips on How To Have A Strong Relationship 22

Chapter 6: *6 Relationship Goals To Have* 28

Chapter 7: **10 Signs You're Falling In Love** 31

Chapter 8: **The 10 signs you aren't ready for a relationship.** 37

Chapter 9: 10 Signs Someone Has A Crush On You 41

Chapter 10: 6 Signs You Have A Fear of Intimacy 47

Chapter 11: 6 Ways On How To Make Your Partner Feel Loved 51

Chapter 12: *Make Time for Your Partner* 54

Chapter 13: **Ten ways men fall in Love.** 56

Chapter 14: 6 Signs You Have Found A Real Friend 62

Chapter 15: 8 Signs That Someone Is Not Your Soulmate 65

Chapter 16: 6 Tips To Find The One 69

Chapter 17: 10 Thoughts That Can Destroy Relationships 73

Chapter 18: 6 Behaviours That Keep You Single 77

Chapter 19: Ten Signs Your Crush Likes You 81

Chapter 20: 7 Signs You Have Found A Keeper 87

Chapter 21: 7 Reasons Why Men Cheat 91

Chapter 22: *7 Ways To Deal With An Overly Jealous Partner* 95

Chapter 23: 5 Signs Someone Only Likes You As A Friend 99

Chapter 24: *5 Ways To Reject Someone Nicely* 102

Chapter 25: 7 Habits To Change Your Life 105

Chapter 1:
10 signs You're In A Healthy Relationship

Good relationships are a prime ingredient for a happy life, and a bad one tends to be a miserable experience. We all know there's plenty of toxic relationships out there. We've seen them, and for many of us, we have been in them. According to a survey, a third of women and a quarter of men have experienced abusive relationships on average.

The term "perfect relationship" is nothing more than a myth. You don't just get one served on a plate. According to a therapist, "One thing healthy relationships largely share is adaptability. They adapt to circumstances because we can't escape the fact that we're always changing and going through different phases in life." It's not a secret that we all have our ups and downs and ebbs and flows, from time to time. And this may as well affect our relationship too. But one shouldn't strive for a perfect relationship; instead, endeavour to make the best one can.

Let's get to the heart of the matter: How do you know that you're in a healthy and robust relationship, or better stated: How do you know you're in a relationship that's good for you? These signs of a healthy relationship may be blazingly obvious, but sometimes we need things written in black and white for us to see that we're on the right path.

1. **You both understand the need for personal space:**

Healthy relationships are all about interdependence; that is, you rely on each other for mutual support but still maintain your identity as a unique individual. A famous saying goes, "Stand together, yet not too near together: For the pillars of the temple stand apart, And the oak tree and the cypress grow not in each other's shadow."

You don't wholly depend on your partner and know that you have a social circle outside of the relationship. Although you're always there for each other, you don't cling to your partner for every little need, and you spend your time pursuing your interests and hobbies too. Having your freedom in a relationship means that your partner should support your life outside the relationship and might not feel the need to know or be involved in every part of your life. And that means giving your partner the same freedom and independence. In other words, your relationship is balanced.

2. **You can talk to each other about anything and everything:**

They say that secrecy is the enemy of intimacy. And every healthy relationship is built on a foundation of honesty and trust. If you trust one another, you can be vulnerable and weak in their company because you recognize that instead of judging you, they will hold you and support you through the dark times. You're able to pour your heart out to them, no matter how stupid some things might sound. You don't keep secrets from each other. And when you're apart, you're not worried about them pursuing other people. You know they won't cheat or lie to you. You're safe and comfortable with them, knowing the fact that they won't ever hurt you, both physically or emotionally. You know they have your best interests in mind and respect you enough to encourage you to make your own choices. In conclusion, you respect each other's privacy, and the element of trust between you two comes naturally, and neither of you goes out of your way to work hard to "earn" their faith.

3. **You support and encourage each other's passions and ambitions:**

If your partner expresses his interest to become Batman, then you should assure that you'll hold the cape for him. If it's essential for them to, it should be important to you too, no matter how strange or bizarre their goals may sound. Even if you don't see eye to eye on something or have plans that aren't the same, healthy relationships are built on mutual inspiration and motivation; your partner should encourage you to be your best self, to face complex challenges, and to change the world, all by being there with you, supporting you through it all.

4. **You accept them for who they are:**

One of the most critical factors contributing to a healthy relationship is that you don't try to fix the other person. Love is all about seeing the flaws and blemishes of your partner and accepting them. It is about abiding by the bad habits and mannerisms of your significant other and working around them. It is about recognizing all the fears and insecurities and reassuring and comforting them. We all go through our bad days. We should strive to hold them in their bad days and dance and celebrate with them in their good ones. None of us are perfect; we're made with cracks and smudges, our souls have been shattered, and our skin is patchwork. There's nothing wrong with that. When your partner is broken, Vow to hold him together, and when your time comes, to be broken, beaten, restless, except that he'll keep you too.

5. <u>Playfulness and Light-heartedness:</u>

Healthy relationships are full of laughter and fun. It all comes down to joking and roasting each other playfully and laughing your hearts out. The spontaneity and adventures that you both might bring would eventually spice up your relationship. Sometimes one of you, or both of you, might feel emotionally or physically drained, or the challenges or distress might affect your relationship's tone. But being able to relieve the tension and share lighter moments, even briefly, strengthens your connection even in tough times.

6. <u>Conflict Resolution:</u>

Even in a healthy relationship, you'll have occasions where you might agree to disagree. It's entirely normal for couples to have disagreements and feel frustrated or angry with their partner. But that doesn't mean you should disrespect your partner based on his opinions and thinking. It all comes down to how you choose to address the conflict. You and your partner must talk about your differences politely, honestly, and with respect. Know when you or your partner is wrong, and apologize rightfully for it. You should be open to change too. Your number 9 might look like a number 6 to your partner, but it doesn't mean your partner is wrong. It simply means you both are looking at the same thing from different perspectives. Couples should try to understand each other, make their points apparent, and then sort out whatever's bothering them.

7. **You feel at ease talking about your past:**

Our past might be filled with our darkest secrets, but it does, in no way, defines us. When you feel free to tell your partner all about your exes, and the time you got depressed, and any failures or rejections that you received in your past, it shows that you trust your partner completely. Everything that has happened to your history has brought you to where you are today and changed you into a completely different person. Your partner should reassure you, and you shouldn't feel the need to hide any details from them. Similarly, you should comfort your partner and give them the same assurance.

8. **You share responsibilities:**

A relationship should always be based on equality. Putting the same effort into the success of the relationship is vital. Yes, sometimes your partner may do their 80%, and you have to put in your 120% and vice versa, but being on the same page and sharing all the responsibilities are a significant sign of a healthy relationship. One of you might be over-responsible in certain things, and one of you might be under-responsible in certain things, and it could be the other way around too. The over/under responsible dynamic is natural. However, when it becomes unbalanced, it can set off a cycle of anger, guilt, hurt, and resentment. Making sure of your particular dynamic and working on your responsibilities allows you to grow as an individual and a couple and balance things out.

9. **Making your partner feel loved:**

You value your partner's emotions and make them feel accepted and important. You ask them about their day, tell them about yours, and listen attentively to whatever they have to say. You both spend quality time together and make memories that you know you'll cherish forever. You never hesitate to try new things with them, maybe go to a restaurant you guys never go to before or go on a spontaneous trip to another city or country. It might be a shared hobby, too, like joining a dance class, jogging daily, or sitting over a cup of coffee. You surprise each other with dates and gifts. And even though the gift might not be that expensive, your partner will hold onto it forever.

10. **Your relationship has gotten stronger over time:**

The ultimate sign that your relationship is sustainable for the long term is that it only grew stronger with time. No matter how many times your partner has pissed you off or annoyed you, you couldn't help but fall in love with them a little more every day. Your relationship has slowly built, developing deeper roots with each passing year. The great David Foster Wallace once said, "The essential kind of freedom involves attention and awareness and discipline, and being able to care about other people truly and to sacrifice for them over and over in myriad petty, unsexy ways every day."

In conclusion, if you relate to the signs above, consider yourself lucky and cling to your partner for as long as your destiny would allow.

If you found this video helpful, don't forget to like, subscribe, comment, and share this with someone important to you. I hope you learned something valuable today. Take care, have a good rest, and till the next video ☺

Chapter 2:

8 Signs You Were Actually In Love

Falling in love is something some of us might have experienced, but others? They might be new to this feeling, and they might not even know its love. There is no way someone could tell you are in love except for you. Unlike disney princesses, a bird isn't going to come flying and whisper it in your ear. You have to check the facts and feelings in this case. Initially, love will feel very exciting and adventurous, but eventually, you will be settled and calm. Love is a colorful feeling. And here are some ways you can make sure that what you feel towards someone is love.

1. You feel thrilled around them:

When the person you like excites you and makes you feel ecstatic. Then you got it. You are in love with them. But don't be so sure right away; it can be affected by adrenaline rushes in your body. But mostly, it's the feeling of butterflies fluttering in your stomach and doing somersaults. Your excitement is not expected but above average.

2. You want to see them again and again:

Even if they have just left, you always wait to see them again. You wait for the hours where you will see them. If you, by any reason, have to see them daily, then except for getting boring, it gets exciting and interesting day by day. Even though it's not healthy to not let them leave, you must calm down. It is common in love.

3. You always smile around them:

It's hard to stay severe and uptight when someone you love is around. So, whenever they make a conversation with you, you always smile. You visit happily around them, and that makes your mood go up a thousand folds. When you enjoy being around someone, it's natural. Just make sure to keep that jaw in check.

4. You see the good in them:

When we fall in love with someone, all we see is the good in them. Their sound quality becomes the highlight of their personality, and their flaws seem small and irrelevant. You ignore their bad habits because of one good quality they might have because, in love, flaws don't matter. The good always attracts people, and that is what might have tempted you towards them and forward with love with them.

5. Imagining a future with them:

We can't imagine a future with anyone we see and get attracted to. But when you start to imagine a lot with someone, it's apparent that you want to spend it with them. You might want to make them a part of your real life. And it can also happen with a bit of effort and communication. It will work out in the end.

6. You change yourself a little:

Shaping yourself according to someone's need sure sounds unhealthy, but it's a true sign of love. When you do things that they might like and make yourself acknowledged by them, then you want their attention all to yourself. You dress nicely, you put on makeup, and talk more confidently. These are all the basics you do to impress them with your charm and your will to make them fall in love with you.

7. You are overprotected by them:

You have a hawk-like gaze on everyone that watches over your love interest. Especially your same gender. Possessiveness is fine until it becomes extreme. You know all the people who talk to them and ensure that some particular stay away from them. We all understand this level of love, and it is okay to be overprotective of your loved one.

8. You change your priorities:

When you change your sense of style and mindset, it's evident that next in the line is the priority. They come a level higher every time they do the minimum for you. And eventually, you won't even notice, and they are much higher on that list to ignore. That is why keeping them a priority changes many aspects of your life, making you happy for the good.

Conclusion:

Falling in love is harmless and colorful. It's exciting and wholesome. All the words might not be enough to describe it, but it's a good feeling. You have to accept that you are in love with a person and need to do something about it. You need to let them know and believe your feelings, and you never know? They might feel the same.

Chapter 3:

6 Ways To Flirt With Someone

No matter how confident and bold we assume ourselves to be, we tend to freeze up and utter a wimpy 'hey' when we see our crush approaching us. Flirting doesn't always come easily to everyone, and there's always struggle, awkwardness, and shyness that follows. But, some people are natural-born flirters and just get the dating thing right.

Knowing how to flirt and actually showing someone that you're interested in them sexually or romantically can be a minefield. But once you get your hands on it, you'll probably become an expert in no time. If you struggle with flirting, we've got some tips to help you master the art of flirting and getting your crush's attention. Below are some ways to flirt with someone successfully.

Be Confident But Mysterious

There's nothing sexier than someone who has a lot of confidence. Of course, I'm not talking about being too overconfident, and it will tend to push people away from you. But if you're strutting down the halls as you own them, your crush (and everyone else) will notice you. Don't give away too much of yourself while being confident. People tend to get intrigued by someone who gives off mysterious vibes. They show their interest in you and avail every opportunity to try to get to know you better. This will lead to you having a chance to make up a good conversation with your crush and even flirt with them in between.

Show That You're Interested In Their Life

Who doesn't love compliments and talking about themselves all the time? We come along with people who mostly like to talk than to listen. If you get a chance to talk to your crush, don't waste it. Ask them questions about their life, get to know their views and ideas about certain things like politics, fashion, controversies, show that you're genuinely interested in them. They will love your curious nature and would definitely look forward to having another conversation with you. This will also give your brownie points of getting to know them better.

Greet Them Whenever You Pass Them

Seeing your crush approach you or simply seeing them standing in the halls can be the scariest feeling ever. You will probably follow your gut reaction and become nervous; either you'll walk past them hurriedly or look down at your phone and pretend like you're in the middle of a text conversation battle. But you have to ignore those instincts, and you have to look up at them and simply smile. You don't have to indulge yourself in an extensive conversation with them. Just taking a second to wave or say hi can be more than enough to get yourself on your crush's radar, as you will come off as polite to them.

Make Ever-So-Slight Contact

The sexiest touches are often those electric ones that come unexpectedly, not the intentional ones that might make someone uncomfortable.

Unnecessary touches can be a turn-on because they signal a willingness to venture beyond the safe boundaries that we usually maintain between ourselves and others. But be careful not to barge into them accidentally. Small, barely-there touches that only the two of you notice are the best. Let your foot slightly touch theirs or lightly brush past them.

Compliment Them

While everyone loves receiving compliments, try not to go overboard, or they would be more likely to squirm in their seat rather than ask you out. You should compliment them lightly about their outfit or fragrance or their features or personality, but keep the subtle flirtation for when the time and moment is right. Giving them compliments would make them think that you're interested in them and want to step up the equation with them.

Look At Them

Experts suggest that we look and then look away three times to get someone's attention. According to the Social Issues Research Centre, maintaining too much eye contact while flirting is people's most common mistake. Our eyes make a zigzag motion when we meet someone new - we look at them from eye to eye and then the nose. With friends, we look below their eye level to include the nose and mouth. The subtle flirt then widens that triangle to incorporate parts of the body. Please don't stare at someone too intensely, or else you'll end up making them feel uncomfortable.

Conclusion

It might seem nerve-wracking to put yourself out there and start flirting, but fear not! It's normal to get nervous around someone whom you like. Follow the above ways to seem confident and pull off a successful flirtation. Know the importance of keeping a balance between revealing your feelings and keeping the person you like intrigued.

Chapter 4:
6 Ways To Deal With Rude People

Rudeness is not a quality everybody likes; on the contrary, most people tend to stay away from rude people, so they don't have to deal with them, but sometimes, we haven't got any options, avoiding them isn't an option. You can meet rude people in your work offices, schools, colleges, or any public place. You have to deal with them. When someone is disrespectful to us, all we want to do is snap back at them, but that would make you just like them. Here are a few ways to deal with rude people.

1. Try To Be Understanding

We have got those bad days when we don't want to talk to anyone and when someone talks to us, we respond a bit rudely even if we don't realize it. The person who's being rude to you could also be going through something right now. The best you can do is be understanding and give them some space. Eventually, they would realize and would apologize. If they don't apologize and continue being rude, just let it go; you can't change how someone wants to talk to people. Everybody has their habits. Even though being rude is not that good practice, it is still a habit, and to change a pattern, a person needs time and willpower.

2. Call Them Out On Their Behavior

As mentioned before, sometimes we don't realize when we ate being rude to someone, but that doesn't make us wrong. It is just that we are going through a particular phase in our life that causes us to be that way. So if someone is rude to you, call them out on their rudeness; if they care, they will indeed apologize. If they don't want to be sorry, then don't get upset, limit your contact with them, like talking to them only when necessary because it's difficult to completely stay away from that rude person if he is a co-worker or a neighbor.

3. Don't Backbite

Don't talk bad about that person behind his back to someone else. Firstly it would spread rumors, and people would not hesitate to gossip. Secondly, talking behind someone's back is also considered rude, so if you talk behind that person's back, what is the difference between you and that rude person. Thirdly, when you talk bad about someone, it will only cause the situation to get worse than it already is.

4. Avoid The Rude Person

Even when you call them out on your behavior but the person is still impolite towards you, don't stress; walk away. If they are rude, then it is their problem, not yours. You don't have you worry about it because there is nothing you can do. Just walk away and don't give that person the slightest chance to talk to you. Indeed, when everyone starts walking away from him, he would realize that this habit is not causing any good and would make an effort to change and become better.

5. Be More Kind

This way is more than complex, of course; who would want to be nice to someone who isn't nice to you, but when you offer some extra kindness, you will set an example for that person. Everybody loves a kind person. After a while of your service, the person would realize that you are kind and don't deserve his rudeness. The other person would eventually calm down and surely will follow your lead. It's hard to be rude to someone who is too kind towards you.

6. Rudeness Is Nothing New

Since the beginning of time, rudeness has been a part of human nature; there is nothing new. No matter what you do, you will always find rude people everywhere you go. All you need to do is accept that this is nothing new and you can't change the way these people think, maybe it is their habit, and perhaps they will change this with time, but there is nothing you can do about it, so don't fret.

Conclusion

Don't take the words of rude people to heart. The world is full of rudeness; no matter what you do, you can't get rid of them. But there is one thing you can do, be the kind and loving person that you are. Don't be rude to them, just be kind towards them. Indeed with time, everybody realizes their bad habits. And don't worry about it, at least you are not among the rude people.

Chapter 5:
9 Tips on How To Have A Strong Relationship

Who doesn't want a strong relationship? Everyone wants to have that high-level understanding with their partner that lasts a lifetime. It is scientifically proven that people who are in healthy relationships have less stress and more happiness.

Healthy relationship not only helps us increase our overall feelings of happiness, but stress-reduction also helps us improve our overall quality of physical and mental health that make every-day life more pleasing to go through. Relationships can be in the form of family, work, friendships, and also romantic ones. Depending on the area that matters the most to you at this very point in your life, you can choose to focus on that specific one until you feel you are ready to focus on the next.

If building powerful relationships is a priority of yours as it is mine, then stay with me till the end of this video because we will be discussing **9 Magical** Tips on How To Have A Strong Relationship with whoever you want. Let's Begin.

Number one
Listen to Each Other
This is the first and probably the most important thing that you might want to take note of. Just think, how many arguments have you had that

went in the wrong direction just because no one was willing to simply just listen? In order to understand each other's point of view both parties must be willing to open up their ears instead of their mouths first. You need to have the stamina to listen to their side of the story before airing yours.

If you truly want a healthy relationship then the foundations starts with a good listening ear. To listen not only when the other party have problems in their lives, but also when they have a problem with you. Develop a good sense of compassion and empathy in the process.

Bitter thoughts, grudge-holding, and negativity toward the other person only serve to weaken your relationships, not strengthen them. So try to understand each other, let the other person speak, and then sort things out in the best possible way.

Number two
Give Time For The Relationship To Grow

For any relationship to truly blossom, it is important to spend the necessary quality time together. Whether the relationship is with family members, friends, or lovers, it takes energy and effort nonetheless. Any amount of energy you spend on that person will reap its benefits later. Now, I am not saying to drastically change your life or to go on adventures or expensive dates to make your relationship healthy. All you have to do is simply get yourself free for a day or night once a week and do something different together, like having a date night, playing games, cooking and eating, watching movies or whatever you like, just give your best at that time. Be present with them and don't be distracted checking your phone or replying work messages.

Number three
Give Time To Yourself

Now I needed to talk about this one right after the number two. I think a good relationship should be balanced. In the previous point, I talked about spending quality time in relationships, but I also don't mean that you should give all your energy to them or stop doing things that energizes your soul. Don't sacrifice your own hobbies for the sake of others. I agree that you need to take more initiative in relationships but at the same time you need to take care of your own happiness too. So give time to yourself and spend it doing things that fills your soul with happiness and gratefulness. You will feel recharged and fresh as a result when you engage in your relationships.

Number four
Learn To Appreciate Little Things

This point will touch more on the romantic relationship side of things. If you are in a relationship for quite a while then there is a chance that you might get complacent and too comfortable. You might also gradually forget the little things that make the person special. As a result the other person could potentially feel like you may be taking them for granted. To avoid this, you need to start making it a constant reminder to yourself to appreciate the little things your partner does for you. Say "I love you" to them, give cute little gifts, give them surprises and tell them how much they mean to you. You need to show your partner how much you love them so they never feel taken for granted. So yeah, start doing all this and make your bond strong!!

Number five
Learn To Forgive

It is well said, "relationships require a lot of forgiveness". As I mentioned earlier, bitter thoughts and grudge-holding just hurt your relationship in the long run. So if you want a happy relationship then you should learn to forgive. If there is something on your mind that your partner did and you can't forget then sit and talk to them about it and try to come up with a good solution. If any of you makes any mistake, you should forgive them with a smiling face and tell them that these little mistakes can't lessen your love. Work on yourself, make your heart ready for what you see coming and even what you don't see coming, and let things go in the right direction. You need to make your heart learn to forgive, this is the only key.

Number Six
Don't expect your partner to complete you

You should be confident about whatever you have. If you are looking for a healthy relationship then you should not expect your partner to complete you. Sometimes, we expect things from our partners which we lack and it can put a strain on your relationship. What you could do instead is to constantly work on yourself to the point that you feel you truly and rightfully deserving of every good thing that comes your way. That you feel secure and independent at the same time in the relationship. Loving yourself first goes a long way in maintaining a strong and healthy relationship with others.

Number Seven
Ways Of Showing Love

Different people show and receive love in their own unique ways. Understanding how the other party expresses or receives love is the key to building a strong relationship. Some people do it by caring for you while others express it through physical affection like hugs and kisses. If you don't know that the specific love language is between you and the other party then it might cause problems in the long run. To really ensure the other party feels loved you have to express it in the way that they receive the most strongly. Go find out what they are by asking them and then start giving it right away!

Number eight
Be Flexible

If you want a healthy relationship then you have to learn to be flexible as well. Flexible in the face of any changes that might occur in your relationship. It is a known fact that change is the only constant in life. We may never be prepared but we should do our best to adapt to new situations that we may find ourselves in. It is also therefore unrealistic not to expect our relationships to change as time progresses as well. Learn to adapt and grow in this new stage and you will be all the more happier for it.

Number nine

Make Decisions Jointly

A good and healthy relationship requires listening to each others' desires and concerns. While you may not always love to do the things that the other party wants, you should always try to find a compromise that suits both of your needs. Instead of insisting and making decisions all the time, try making decisions together that both of you will find enjoyable. Be it where to hang out, what to eat for a meal, where to go on a trip together, or even what kinds of products to buy for your home, make sure that the other party's points of view is heard so that they don't end up resenting you over the long run.

So that's it, guys, we are done with our today's topic of 9 Tips on How To Have A Strong Relationship. Now, it's time for you to share your thoughts. What do you think about these tips? Have you already tried them and do they work? And if you know some other tips to make relationships strong then share them in the comment box to help others. If you got value then smash the like button and don't forget to subscribe to our channel as we will be talking about some amazing topics in the future. See you soon!

Chapter 6:
6 Relationship Goals To Have

We live in a generation where the term "relationship goals" has become a part of the trendy vernacular. It may seem more like a hashtag than anything else, but we all are eager to go into the depth of its meaning. A beautiful photo of a stunning couple having a good time together? Relationship goals. A cute text message sent to a girlfriend from his boyfriend? Relationship goals. A perfect wedding? Relationship goals. All these might seem sweet and enviable and look like an absolute dream, and it doesn't mean that these come off as accessible to them. If you have ever been in a relationship, you would know exactly what I'm saying.

Love is not always fireworks, passion, and butterflies. Relationships are not just date nights, kisses, and cuddles. And love is not that glamorous as it looks on social media. But when you strive to build something together, involving your selflessness, commitment, and even sweat and tears, those are actual relationship goals. Here is a list of what relationship goals you must have with your partner.

1. Always Do New Things Together

Sure, alone time might be great, but together time is where the magic happens too. Avoiding your relationship becoming mundane and a rut, you both should try to do new things together. This could be choosing any vacation spot or having an exciting adventure together. You both should make a list of all the things you want to do with each other and keep adding stuff that might pop later. Tick things off as you go, and you'll never run out of things to do together.

2. Be Each Other's Biggest Supporters

Perhaps one of the best things about being in a relationship is that you'll always have someone in your corner. Regardless of how crazy or unrealistic your dreams and goals may sound, your partner should be your biggest supporter. Seeing the person you love believing in could come off as a massive motivation to achieve your goals. This goes both ways; both men and women need to feel emotionally supported. You both should take some time out to discuss what emotional support looks like to you, what and when you need it, and then provide the said support for each other.

3. Put Each Other First

Putting each other first in your relationship will ensure that you're paying attention to each other's needs and making sure they are being met. You have become selfless with each other, and you both strive to make each other happy and would do anything to put a smile on each other's faces. You complement each other, protect each other, support and love each other, no matter the obstacles or circumstances.

4. Know The Importance of Alone Time

As much as you don't want to keep your hands off your partner in the early stages of your relationship, it's essential to know that you both need time alone to recharge and refill your cup. Spending all of your time together isn't sustainable, and alone time is significant. It will help you maintain your individuality, allow you breathing space, and encourage a closer relationship with each other when you spend time together.

5. Keep The Physical Connection Going

Sex isn't always an option when dealing with different phases of your relationship. There are going to be times when it might not be physically or mentally possible. But this in no way means that you should stop all physical connections. Physically touching the person you love releases an oxytocin hormone; this feel-good love hormone reduces stress and makes you feel wonderful things. You can stay physically connected by holding hands, cuddling, or simply leaning on one another.

6. Speak Positively About Each Other

Speaking ill of your partner with others is not only disrespectful to them, but it's also disrespectful to your relationship. Sure, you can vent in tough times, but make sure you talk about the actions and behaviors that upset you and not their personality traits. Always speak positively and kindly of each other. Even if their behavior irritates you, focus more on the characteristics you love of them and let it pass.

Conclusion

Relationships are complicated but beautiful at the same time. As simple as the above factors may sound to you, these things take a lot of effort and hard work to be implemented. But when you do all of these with the person you love the most in the world, then all of it can be worth it.

Chapter 7:

<u>10 Signs You're Falling In Love</u>

As our Literature master, Shakespeare, once said, 'A heart to love, and in that heart, courage, to make's love known.'

Ah, love! A four-lettered small word that leaves such a heavy impact on people. Falling in love is nothing short of a beautiful experience, but it can also give you a veritable roller-coaster of emotions. From feeling unsure to terrifying, disgusting, exhilarating, and excited, you might feel it all. If your mobile screen pops up and you're hoping to see their name on the screen, or you're looking for their face in a crowd full of thousands, then you, my child, are doomed! You are well familiar with the feeling of getting butterflies just by hearing their voice, the urge to change your wardrobe completely to impress them, the constant need to be with them all the time. It is known that people who are in love tend to care about the other person's needs as they do their own.

You often go out of their way for their happiness. Whether it's something as small as making their favorite dish or impressing them with some grand gestures, you always try to make them feel content and happy.

If you're in the middle of some casual inquiry into whether you're falling in love, then we are here to help you. Below are some signs for you to discover if it's really just simply a loss of appetite or if you're merely lovesick.

1. **You don't hesitate to try new things with them:**

One of the factors that you could look into is that you become fearless and more adventurous when you are in love. You don't hang back to step out of your comfort zone and engage in all your partner favors' activities and interests. Suddenly the idea of trying sushi or wearing something bright doesn't seem so crazy. You are willing to be more daring and open to new experiences. You are ready to go on that spontaneous trip with them and make memories, all while being a little scared inside. But isn't love all about trying new things with your partner? The New York Times article in 2008 revealed that people in a relationship who try new hobbies together help keep the spark alive long after the honeymoon phase is over.

2. **You're always thinking about them:**

When you are in love, you always tend to think about your partner. Rehash your last conversation with them, or simply smiling at something they said, or questions like what they must be doing right now, have they eaten their meal yet, did they go to work on time or were late again, are always on the back of your mind. You are mentally, emotionally, and physically impacted about caring for them. But it isn't overwhelming. Instead, you get a sense of a calm and secure reality that you will constantly crave. When in love, we tend to merge with that person in such a way that they start to dominate our thoughts and we become wholly preoccupied with them.

3. **You become anxious and stressed:**

According to a psychology study, falling in love could also cause higher levels of cortisol, a stress home, in your body. So the next time you feel jittery or anxious, that person might mean more to you than you think. You might become anxious to dress up nicely to impress them, or if they ask you something, the pressure of answering them intellectually can be expected. But suppose you're feeling overly anxious about your partner, like them not texting you back instantly or thinking they might be cheating on you. In that case, it's an indication of insecure attachment, and you might want to work on yourself to avoid feeling like this.

4. **You become inspired and motivated:**

A few days ago, you needed the motivation to get out of bed. And now, the future suddenly seems so bright and full of potential. Your partner inspires you to set up new goals, have a positive attitude, and cheer you from behind while you feel full of energy and chase them. When we are in love, a part of our brain, considered the reward system, releases excess dopamine, and we feel invincible, omnipotent, and daring. Your life becomes significantly better when you're around them.

5. **You become empathetic towards them:**

It's not a secret that you start seeing your partner as an extension of yourself and reciprocate whatever they feel when you fall in love. Suppose they are accepted into their favorite program, or they expect to receive that interview call, or their favorite football team might have lost in the quarters. In that case, you might feel the same excitement, happiness, or distress that your partner does. Becoming empathetic towards your partner means making sacrifices for them, like going to the grocery store because your partner is tired or refueling their tank in the cold so that they don't have to step out. According to an expert, "Your love is growing when you have an increased sense of empathy toward your partner. When they feel sad, you feel sad. When they feel happy, you feel happy. This might mean going out of the way to give them love in the way that they want to receive it, even if it is not the way you would want to receive love."

6. **It's just plain easy:**

You don't have to put in extra effort, and it doesn't seem to drain your energy. Instead, you feel energized and easy. You can be your complete, authentic self around them. And it always just seems to go with the flow. Even the arguments don't feel much heated as they did in the other relationships. When you're in love, you prioritize your partner over your pride and ego. You don't hesitate to apologize to them and keep your relationship above everything. When you are with your partner, and it doesn't feel like hard work, know that they are the one!

7. **You crave their presence:**

Some theorists say that we are more drawn to kissing, hugging, and physical touch when we fall in love. Physical closeness releases a burst of the love hormone termed Oxytocin, which helps us feel bonded. Of course, you don't want to come as someone too clingy who is permanently attached to his partner's hip, but knowing where your person is or how their day went is what you should be looking forward to. On the flipside, Corticotrophin is released as part of a stress response when we are away from our partner, which can contribute to anxiety and depression.

8. You feel safe around them:

It takes a lot of courage for people to open up to their partners. If you don't mind being vulnerable around them, or if you've opened up to them about your dark past or addressed your insecurities, and they have listened contently to you and reassured you. You have done vice versa with your partner, then that's just one of the many signs that you both are in love with each other. Long-lasting love gives you a solid ground and a safe space where you can be upset and vulnerable. When we feel an attachment to our partner, our brain releases the hormones vasopressin and Oxytocin, making us feel secure.

9. You want to introduce them to your family and friends:

You just never shut up about your love interest over the family dinner or when hanging out with your friends. They know all about them, from their favorite spot in the city to the color of their eyes, to how much you adore them and want to spend every single minute talking about them. And now all your family members and friends are curious to meet the guy/girl they have been listening about for the past few weeks. You want to introduce them into every aspect of your life and want it to last this time. So, you make perfect arrangements for them to meet your friends and family, and on the other hand, threatens them to behave Infront of him/her.

10. You care about their happiness:

When you put them and their feelings first, that's how you know it's true love. You don't just want happiness for yourself only, but instead wants it in excess measure for your partner. According to marriage researchers at UC Berkeley, " Spouses who love each other stay together longer, be happier, and support each other more effectively than couples who do not love each other compassionately." You want to go out of your way, or do their favorite thing, to see a smile on their face.

Conclusion:

If you relate to the signs above, then you've already been hit by the love cupid. Scientists have discovered that falling in love, is in fact, a real thing. The brain releases Phenylethylamine, a hormone known for creating feelings of infatuation towards your significant other. The mix and match of different hormones released in our body while we are in love are wondrous. If you have gotten lucky and found a special someone for yourself, then cling to them and don't let them go! If you found this video helpful, please like and subscribe to the channel. Also don't forget to share this video with someone who you find might benefit from this topic as well!

Chapter 8:
The 10 signs you aren't ready for a relationship.

Relationships can be complicated sometimes, but what makes them more complicated is we ourselves. There are times when we fail to understand when to step back and think in a different way about life. We often fail to understand where we stand and where the relationship should stand leading to a lot of anxiety and pain in the long run. Sometimes it's more important to step out of the flow and give yourself time to think about things deeper.

Here are 10 signs that show you might not be ready for a relationship just yet at this very moment:

1. When you aren't happy with your own self.

We often feel a relationship or another person can make us happy, but unfortunately, unless you are happy with your own self, no one can come and make you happy. As the saying goes, happiness is within. It is very important to first find what makes you happy in life and gives you freedom. Because unless we know how to make ourselves happy, we cannot be at peace with another person too.

2. When you feel a relationship will help you overcome your loneliness.

We all do get lonely sometimes. But a relationship isn't the solution for overcoming that. When we expect another person to help us get past the loneliness it just creates a lot of pressure on the other person and might end up suffocating them too. Read a good book, make some nice dinner, watch that favorite rom-com alone, get that pet which you always wanted, because you need to be your best friend first and when you know how to overcome your loneliness, the other person will love your company too.

3. When you aren't sure about the person and jumped into the relationship faster than you wanted to.

As much as it is important for someone to understand themselves, it is also very important for us to know the person we are planning on getting in a relationship with. Do you see that person with you 10 years down the lane? Is he the one you had dreamt your life with? A relationship is a two-way street. It is very important to express and set your standards and expectations in the relationship clear.

4. When you still aren't healed from your past.

We all have a past. Some memories are good some still give us nightmares, but it is very important to consider it as just a life lesson and move on. The more we stick to our past, the more distant we get from our future dreams and goals. If you keep thinking about how your ex broke the promises and cheated on you, you won't be able to see the good intentions of the current person who probably could have been there in the future too, but you couldn't be completely happy with them based on your past instincts.

5. When you have fear of commitments and the idea of making sacrifices pushes you away.

We all have fears inside of us. Fear of how things will turn out in the future, we get apprehensive of taking a serious step in life. Commitment should be given only when you are ready from inside because for any relationship to work out both of you should be on the same page and only when your heart tells you are ready!

6. When you have a lot of insecurities and self-doubts.

No one likes to stay with a person who is full of self-doubts and always needs validation for everything in life. You need to be confident about your own self first because only then you can grow in the relationship and motivate the other person to grow too. Too many insecurities come in when there is not enough communication and when you cannot openly express your fears to the person.

7. When the relationship is not motivating you to grow into a better version of yourself and boosting your personal growth.

If you find yourself in a relationship where your personal life and growth are stagnant, then you are with the wrong person. As much as you should be investing in the other person it is also very important to invest in yourself and help the other person invest in themselves too. If the relationship doesn't motivate you to achieve that dream, get that dream house one day, travel together to the favorite destination, have that dream cruise, and get the dream car together, then you might as well feel the need to rethink why is it so.

8. When you feel situations are one-sided in the relationship.

Sometimes we end up with people who are not as much into us as we are into them. Their efforts and actions don't match their words. So it is very important to be vocal about your expectations in the relationship and not stay in one just for the sake of being in a relationship. Along with love, understanding the sentiments, emotions, and vulnerabilities of a person is also very important and if the person is not matching up to the mark, life is too short to give chances to a person who won't care as much as you would.

9. When you get hindered in communicating openly.

Open communication is very important for a healthy relationship. If you are having inhibitions about talking about your problems and insecurities to the person, either because you feel they won't understand you or because any discussion with the person ends up in an argument, then quite understandably you are with the wrong person and need to get yourself out of the relationship.

10. Peer pressure and wrong decisions.

This happens for marriages too. Any kind of relationship should not happen under pressure. If it's because all your friends are engaged and/or committed to someone, doesn't necessarily mean you have to do the same. There are many more things to experience in life. Unless you really want to get along with someone, you shouldn't go in it just because you feel cornered and lonely among your friends. Make better choices and better stories to tell them and make them feel jealous of your single but happy life! ;)

So That's It For Today's Video. If you found this helpful, don't forget to like, subscribe, comment, and share this with someone important to you. I hope you learned something valuable today. Take care, have a good rest, and till the next video ☺

Chapter 9:
10 Signs Someone Has A Crush On You

Have that inkling suspicion that someone likes you but you're not 100% sure about it?

Many of you will agree that there is a certain level of thrill and adrenaline rush when it comes to crushing on someone. It could also lead to feelings of anxiety and nervousness as well.

I'm sure you've been in a similar situation before – where you had a crush on someone and not know how to express or be yourself around that person. But at the same time secretly hoping he or she knows you're attracted to them so that you may begin a romantic relationship with them.

What if you're on the receiving end of that crush, how do you identify the signs and signals that the person is sending you?

Here are 10 Signs that someone has a crush on you:

1.There is a distinct difference in their behavior when they are around you.

It may not be obvious or easily noticeable, but the guy or girl who is secret crushing on you will most likely be nervous when they are around you, or when they engage you in conversation. They might act shy or coy, and maybe even blush when looking at you.

On the flip side, they might also be more enthusiastic in their approach towards you - by expressing cheerfulness because one some level, you make them happy. A person who likes you will pay more attention to the minor details of what you say and what you do. They might also try to make sure you feel great because they want you to feel comfortable and at ease around them as well.

2. They might notice you from a distance.

A person who has a crush on you will likely try to peek a gaze at you from a distance. Whether you are at the same workplace, gym, or friendly hangouts with other friends, if you catch them looking at you more than usual, that is a very big sign that is pointing in your favor. They are also likely to spend a longer time gazing at you or giving you some serious eye contact.

In the digital age, distance could also be in the form of internet presence. They might also try to look you up on your social media channels. A good way to tell is if they start liking your posts and commenting on them. That is their way of entering into your life without being too obvious about it.

3. They will always find excuses to come close or talk.

You can easily understand whether someone is interested in you or not by their enthusiasm for interacting with you. Whether it is trying to match their timings for going to the coffee break with you or adjusting their dates with their friends to take you out to the movie, they will never leave one opportunity to chance to spend that golden time with you. They might also find the silliest of reason for just starting a conversation with you - like asking whether you will teach them something new or bring them somewhere for a meal.

4. Everything you do is appreciated by them.

As a crush, their goal is to make you notice them. To show you that they deserve your attention and time.

If you are going through a bad day, count on your potential crush to talk to you or to make an effort to help you feel better. It is highly likely that your crush will try their best to encourage and make you laugh as well.

They might also laugh at your silliest of jokes. Take it as a form of flattery as it shows that they want to win you over. At the end of the day, as long as it is genuine, it is always better to be around someone who helps you feel good at the end of the day.

5. Lets you know they are always available when you need them.

Another sign that your crush likes you is that they will make themselves available to you as and when you might want to talk. They might be quick to reply your messages when you text them, and they will find time for you whenever they can to engage you in conversations that lets them get to know you more. They might also throw in some hints there to show their interest in you.

6. Makes excuses to touch you!

If someone has a crush on you, they will definitely express interest by engaging in physical contact with you. Be it just as an excuse to feel the soft sweat shirt you are wearing or turning your wrist to appreciate your watch, watch out for these signs. Physical touch is a sign of flirting, and you need to pay attention to them. If they go one step further by poking you or touching you from the back, it is a sure-fire way to know that your someone likes you.

7. Surprise you!

This might not happen with everyone, but there are some people who likes the art of gifting! Especially when they like someone they want to make them feel special, be it bringing them their favorite chocolates and flowers, treating you to a meal, buying you your favorite drink, or getting you something you told them you liked during the last conversation. These are signs that they are paying attention to the little details about you, and that they are trying to express their attraction for you in the form of gift-giving. Friends don't usually buy things for you for no reason at all, so pay attention to this!

8. Borrowing things.

This sign may be rare as well but it could happen. It may sound cliché but when we like someone, we want to keep their things close to us. Any items which belong to you will be special to the person who likes you! Borrowing things could be their way of engaging in interaction with you as well, especially if they are very shy to ask you out.

9. They Compliment your appearance and dressing.

An easy way to know if someone has a crush on you is if they have nice compliments for the clothes you are wearing, for the styling of your hair, or just simply saying you look good today. We say the same when we go on dates to someone we find attractive. We give them compliments to show the other party that we are interested in them. The next time you receive a compliment from someone you suspect has a crush on you, take note of this point.

10. They Ask You Out

If your crush likes you, he or she will most likely ask when you are free to go for a meal or to watch a movie together. They might want to take this time to get you to notice them as more than friends. If they engage in any of the previous 9 signs we have discussed, you could potentially be on a date without even knowing it. So watch out for the signs carefully!.

If however, you are emotionally unavailable, it is perfectly okay to let your crush know at any point that you are not ready for a relationship if you see it being a potential cause of issue for your friendship with them. Ensure that you first confirm that they do indeed have a crush on you before you take any drastic actions to reject them if you are uninterested.

Now that you know what those signs are, you will know how to respond if someone has a crush on you. Do what you will with the information, just do go breaking too many hearts!

Chapter 10:

6 Signs You Have A Fear of Intimacy

Intimacy avoidance or avoidance anxiety, also sometimes referred to as the fear of intimacy, is characterized as the fear of sharing a close emotional or physical relationship with someone. People who experience it do not consciously want to avoid intimacy; they even long for closeness, but they frequently push others away and may even sabotage relationships for many reasons.

The fear of intimacy is separate from the fear of vulnerability, though both of them can be closely intertwined. A person who has a fear of intimacy may be comfortable becoming vulnerable and showing their true self to their trusted friends and relatives. This problem often begins when a person finds relationships becoming too close or intimate. Fear of intimacy can stem from several causes. Overcoming this fear and anxiety can take time, but you can work on it if you know the signs of why you have the fear in the first place.

1. **Fear Of Commitment**

A person who has a fear of intimacy can interact well with others initially. It's when the relationship and its value grow closer that everything starts to fall apart. Instead of connecting with your partner on an intimate level, you find ways and excuses to end the relationship and replace it with yet another superficial relationship. Some might even call you a 'serial dater,' as you tend to lose interest after a few dates and abruptly end the relationship. The pattern of emerging short-term relationships and having a 'commitment phobia' can signify that you fear intimacy.

2. Perfectionism

The idea of erfectionism often works to push others away rather than draw them near. The underlying fear of intimacy often lies in a person who thinks he does not deserve to be loved and supported. The constant need for someone to prove themselves to be perfect and lovable can cause people to drift apart from them. Absolute perfectionism lies in being imperfect. We should be able to accept the flaws of others and should expect them to do the same for us. There's no beauty in trying to be perfect when we know we cannot achieve it.

3. Difficulty Expressing Needs

A person who has a fear of intimacy may have significant difficulty in expressing needs and wishes. This may stem from feeling undeserving of another's support. You need to understand that people cannot simply 'mind read,' they cannot know your needs by just looking at you; this might cause you to think that your needs go unfulfilled and your feelings of unworthiness are confirmed. This can lead to a vicious cycle of you not being vocal about your needs and lacking trust in your partner, and your relationship is meant to doom sooner or later.

4. Sabotaging Relationships

People who have a fear of intimacy may sabotage their relationship in many ways. You might get insecure, act suspicious, and accuse your partner of something that hasn't actually occurred. It can also take the form of nitpicking and being very critical of a partner. Your trust in your partner would lack day by day, and you would find yourself drifting apart from them.

5. Difficulties with Physical Contact

Fear of intimacy can lead to extremes when it comes to physical contact. It would swing between having a constant need for physical contact or avoiding it entirely. You might be inattentive to your partner's needs and solely concentrate on your own need for sexual release or gratification. People with a fear of intimacy may also recoil from sex altogether. Both ends of the spectrum lead to an inability to let go or communicate intimately emotionally. Letting yourself be emotionally naked and bringing up your fears and insecurities to your partner may help you overcome this problem.

6. You're Angry - A Lot

One way that the deep, subconscious fear of intimacy can manifest is via anger. Constant explosions of anger might indicate immaturity, and immature people are not able to form intimate relationships. Everyone gets angry sometimes, and it's an emotion that we cannot ignore, even if we want to. But if you find that your feelings of anger bubble up constantly or inappropriately, a fear of intimacy may be lurking underneath. Don't deny these intimacy issues, but instead put them on the table and communicate effectively with the person you are interested in.

Conclusion

Actions that root out in fear of intimacy only perpetuate the concern. With effort, especially a good therapist, many people have overcome this fear and developed the understanding and tools needed to create a long-term intimate relationship.

Chapter 11:
6 Ways On How To Make Your Partner Feel Loved

The word partner has a deep meaning. It means the association with each other. They understand each other, respecting and supporting every step and decision of each other. In simple words, a partner indicates being fully committed to each other.

Being committed includes many challenges, but one of the biggest and the main challenges is how to make your partner feel loved. This is a big challenge because many partners still don't understand each other entirely after spending most of the time together. Efforts from both partners can help in this situation which can lead to a happy and healthy relationship.

Comforting each other in every situation, mostly in their challenging times, has always played a key role in making your partner feel loved. Your partner knows that you are always there to support them and expressing your willingness to make them relieved, and never doubt their decision.

1. **Complementing Each Other**

Many people think that the female partner in a relationship needs compliments, but the truth is every human being on this planet needs compliments sometimes. Compliments matter a lot, even for boys, but they don't show that they need compliments. Even if they are complimented, they don't show the happiness of being praised. Being praised by a stranger or not so close doesn't matter a lot, but if the compliment comes from an immediate or loved one, it means the world to them.

Complimenting each other back and forth can also improve communication, which is the building block.

2. Be Attentive Towards Each Other

Taking each other for granted destroys a relationship. Instead, try to give all of your attention to your partner. It strengthens a connection. It makes them feel wanted. Listen to them with your complete attention. Listen to the first and then give your opinion or comfort them depending on the situation. Pay him the attention the partner deserves because every moment you spend with him is crucial. Whether planning a dinner or a movie night, always carve out time to be with each other. And when you're spending that quality time together, let things flow naturally and give your partner your undivided attention. Show your interest in them and make them feel that you want to be in their company.

3. Little Gestures of Love

Little gestures can also show your partner how much you care about them and make them feel special and loved. Small gestures can include checking on them, texting them, calling them to say how much you miss them, making plans to meet them, sending small meaningful gifts, asking how their day was and what they are doing tomorrow. Plan surprises for them. Randomly say how much you love them. These small gestures will make their day a hundred percent better.

4. Accept That

Acknowledge your partner. Appreciate them for what they are doing for you. Thank them for their attention and their support, and the love they have given. Thank them just for being there. No one is perfect. Everyone has flaws, and those flaws need to be accepted. A person can never be in front of the person they love until and unless the person they love accepts for who they are and accepts their flaws.

5. Appreciate Them

Make them feel special. Make them feel proud of who you have chosen as a partner. Tell them that it was the right decision to choose them as a partner. Send them appreciation paragraphs. Tell them that they are important and they matter and that you cannot take a step or decision without their opinion. Relive and remember your memories with them. Take a trip down memory lane once in a while. Cherish your happy memories, remember you are bad ones too, and promise each other that no more memories like these will ever be made again. Try not to break promises. Try to fulfill them.

6. Excite Each Other Up

Compliment his accomplishments. Tell him that you are proud of what he accomplished and how hard he worked for those accomplishments. Tell him how he deserved what he accomplished.

Conclusion:

Be abundant with happiness. Let your partner lead. Respect him. Be loyal and faithful and give your hundred percent. Be kind and forgive them. Never let your ego win, and never let pride enter your heart.

Chapter 12:
Make Time for Your Partner

When I first got into my relationship, I thought my boyfriend and my 100-hour workweek would have to battle it out until the bitter end. Yet somehow, I've managed to maintain both. It turns out there are a lot of weird [ways to make time for your partner](#) when you're busy AF. You may have to get creative and resort to some weird measures, but I am living proof that there is no such thing as being too busy for your loved ones.

We all have to run errands. That time is gone from your workday anyway. So, why not use it to show your partner you care instead of just getting what you need? Picking up each other's shampoo and favorite cereal (or, perhaps more practically, take turns picking up groceries and toiletries for the both of you) is one way to connect without needing to make any more time in your schedule.

You spend the same amount of time cooking for two people as you do for one, but since you're feeding two, you *save* time by doing this. Think about it: Instead of cooking every night, you only have to do it every *other* night. Even if you both eat it in front of your computers, making food for each other is a loving gesture that'll make you appreciate each other.

If you live together, you'll probably be sleeping in the same bed anyway. But even if you don't, your dates can consist solely of sleeping if that's what it takes to make time for each other. Or, if you can't sleep through the night with someone else next to you, you can try just sharing nap time.

Even if you don't get around to working out that much, the time you can devote to exercise will help clear your mind, so it's worthwhile if you can make it out for a short run or yoga class. Plus, [working out together can boost your attraction](#) by releasing endorphins.

I can't always handle this, especially when I need to feel like nobody wants my attention to focus. But for less intensive tasks, it can be comforting to cuddle up to your significant other while you're working. You can even be each other's sounding boards if you need help coming up with ideas.

This one will not work for everyone. But if you have an office in a similar place, your walk or ride to work can be your bonding time, even if it's just part of the way. Even just a shared walk to the train station can pay off if you think ahead enough to coordinate your trips to and from work.

Chapter 13:

Ten ways men fall in Love.

Genuine and true Love is so rare that when you encounter it in any form, it's a beautiful thing to be utterly cherished in whatever form it takes. But how does one get this genuine and true Love? Almost every romantic movie, we have seen that a guy meets a girl and, sure enough, falls head over heels for her. But translating that into the real world can be quite a task. The science of attraction works wonders for us. Sometimes we are instantly drawn to some people. On the other hand, we couldn't care less for others. And quite a few times, things flow naturally in our direction, making it all feel surreal and causing butterflies.

A famous psychologist once said: "Love is about an expansion of the self whereby another person's interests, values, social network, and finances become part of your life just as you share your resources with them."

A human mind is, nonetheless, a very complex organ. It can either makes you feel like you're on top of the world with its positive attitude or under it with its negative one. And a male mind, perhaps, seems always like a mystery to us. But it's not such rocket science that we can't get our hands on it. If you're developing feelings for someone and need a bit of guidance to get the man of your dreams to notice you and care about you, then you've just come to the right place!

Here are some ways about what a man needs to fall in Love.

1. **Always Be Yourself:**

Keeping a façade of fake personality and pretending to be someone you're not can be a huge turn-off for men. Instead let the guy know the real you. Let them see who you really are and what you really have to offer. You will not only gain respect from them, but you wouldn't have to keep hiding behind a mask. If you're pretending to be someone else, that only suggests that you're not comfortable with yourself. And many guys will realize this shortcoming and quickly become disinterested. You don't have to dumb down your intellect or put a damper on your exuberant personality. Men like women who are completely honest with them from the start. Who shows them their vulnerable side as well as their opinionated and intelligent one. You're in no need to pretend that your IQ isn't off the charts. Be your genuine, miserable, confident, and independent self always. That way, he will know exactly what he's getting into.

2. **Make him feel accepted and appreciated:**

From a simple thank you text to calling him and asking him about his day, making small gestures for him, and complimenting and praising him, a man needs it all. Men don't always show it, but they are loved to be told that they look good, they're doing a good job, or how intellectual they are. Sometimes men are confused about where women may stand, and they want to see that he's being supported beyond any superficial matter.

When men share glimpses of their inner self with you and put themselves in a vulnerable position, which men rarely do, this is when it's crucial to make him feel rest assured that he will be accepted and appreciated. If women make men feel lifted high and admired, then it's pure magic for them. His heart will make such a deep connection with you that it can only be amplified from thereon.

3. Listen! Don't just talk:

You would see a lot of men complain that they are not heard enough. And quite frankly, it is true. It's essential to establish a mutual balance in the conversation. Women shouldn't make it all about themselves. They need to let the men speak and hear them attentively, and respond accordingly. Ask him questions about his life and his passion, his likes and dislikes. That way, he'll know that you are genuinely interested in him. Men have a lot to say when you show that you can listen. They'll be more inclined to say the things that matter.

4. Laugh out loud with him:

Men tend to make the women of their liking laugh a lot. When you're laughing, you're setting off chemicals in a guy's brain to feel good. Make him feel like he has a great sense of humor, and he's making you happy with his silly and jolly mannerism. Similarly, men are attracted to women who have a spirit that can make them feel good. Tell him enjoyable stories, roast people with him, jump in on his jokes and laugh wholeheartedly with him. He will become attracted to you.

5. **Look your best:**

You don't have to shred a few pounds, or get clear, glowing skin, or change your hairstyle to impress the men of your liking. You have to be confident enough in your skin! Men love a confident woman who feels secure about herself and her appearance. You don't even have to wear body-hugging clothes or tight jeans to make him drool over you (Of course, you can wear them if you want). But a simple pair of jeans and a t-shirt can go a long way too. Just remember to clean yourself up nice, put on nice simple clothes, wear that unique perfume, style up your hair a bit, and voila! You're good to go.

6. **Be trustworthy:**

Another reason that men instantly attract you is when they have the surety that they can trust you with anything and everything. According to love and marriage experts "Trust is not something all loving relationships start with, but successful marriages and relationships thrive on it. Trust is so pervasive that it becomes part of the fabric of these strong relationship." If you want to win a man's heart, reassure him that he can be vulnerable around you and make him feel accepted and secure.

7. **Don't try to change him:**

"He's completely right for me... if only he didn't dress up like that or snore during his sleep."

Sure we might have a few things on our list about how our partner should be, but that doesn't mean we should forcibly try to change their habits. He might have a few annoying habits that will get on your nerves now and then, but that shouldn't be a dealbreaker for you. Instead, we should accept him with all his wits and flaws. You shouldn't just tolerate his little quirks but rather try to admire them too. If something about him is bothering you, try talking to him politely about it. And he might consider changing it for you!

8. Have intellectual conversations with him:

There's nothing that a man finds sexier than women with opinion and intellect. Get his views on a news article, engage him in a heated debate about controversial topics, put your views out the front; even if they clash with his, especially if they conflict with his, he'd be more interested and intrigued about knowing your stance. Show your future partner that you can carry on an intelligent conversation with him anytime he likes.

9. Be patient:

I can't stress enough that patience is perhaps the most vital key to getting a guy to fall for you. It would be best if you gave him time to analyze and process his feelings for you. If you tend to rush him on the subject, you might end up disappointed. Even if you do lose your cool, don't let him know it. Just be patient and consistent, and don't come off as too clingy or needy. If you appear too desperate, it's going to turn him off of the relationship entirely.

10. **Let him know you're thinking of him:**

In the early days of dating, you might be hesitant to tell him that you're thinking of him. You love it when he texts you randomly, saying he's thinking about you, so why not reciprocate it? Invest your time, energy, and efforts in him. Leave him short, sweet notes, or text him in the middle of the day saying that he is on your mind or sending him a greeting card with a cute personal message. Don't overdo it by reminding him constantly if he does not respond. None of these screams' overboard' and are guaranteed to make him smile.

Conclusion:

I hope this article deconstructed and gave you some insights into what makes a man fall for a woman. As the saying goes, 'Men are from mars and women are from Venus and Venus is great, but surely, we need to know about the inner workings of mars too.' Just keep the above tips in mind, be consistent and commit to him considerably, and you're good to go! If you found this video helpful, don't forget to like, subscribe, comment, and share this with someone important to you. I hope you learned something valuable today. Take care, have a good rest, and till the next video ☺

Chapter 14:
6 Signs You Have Found A Real Friend

Life seems easy when we have someone by our side. Everyone makes at least one friend in their life as if it comes naturally. That one person who we can rely on in difficult times. That one person who cares for us when we forget to care for ourselves. Friends are family that we get to choose ourselves. So, we have to decide that person exceptionally carefully. Friends are people who know who you are. You can share both joy and sadness with them without hesitating.

Friends have a significant impact on our lives. They can change us completely and help us shape ourselves into someone better. However, there might be some forgery in your way. Some people consider themselves as your friend, but we fail to notice that it is otherwise. So, it is imperative to choose a friend carefully, while an essential fraction is dependent on our friendship with someone. A good friend is the one whom you can count on to hold you when you require one. A friend is someone who becomes selfless when it comes to us. They always stay by your side as it said, "friends till the end."

1.You Can Be Yourself Around Them
No matter how you behave in front of your family or co-workers, you can always act like yourself in front of your friend. When they give you a sense of comfort, you automatically become yourself. That is the reason

you never get tired of a friend. Because who gets tired of being who they are. A friend is a person who accepts us with all our flaws and stays by us even in our worst phase. They find beauty in your imperfections. That type of friend becomes necessary to keep around.

2. A Support For Good And Bad Times

We all are aware that support is what we want in our time of need. To share our difficult times and to share our good news with someone. A friend listens. They listen to whatever you want to ramble to them without complaining. They understand you and try to give to advice as well as possible. They are an excellent shoulder to cry on. They feel joy in your happiness. They feel sadness in your loss. Friends are people who love us, and thus, we give them ours in return.

3. You Trust Each Other

Trust is an essential foundation in any friendship. Otherwise, you are meant to fall apart. It would help if you grew that trust slowly. When you are loyal to each other, then there is nothing that comes between you two. You need to develop that trust slowly. When you are dedicated to each other, then there is nothing that comes between you two. Honesty is a must when it comes to building your trust with each other. If even one of you is lying about anything, then that friendship fails. Even if they didn't keep their promise, you can't trust them.

4. They Hype You Up

They won't fall back on complimenting you when you look your best. But a friend won't hesitate to confront you if you don't look good. That is what we like about them, and they won't make you look bad in front of others. They will make sure you know you are worth it. They will make you work for what you deserve. Friends will always try to hype you up and will accolade you. They know what you like and don't, so they shape you like you want to be shaped.

5. You Share Almost Everything

Two friends are always together in spirits. When something noteworthy happens in your life, you always feel the need to share it with someone. That someone will probably be a friend. You tend to share every little detail of any event of your life with them comfortably. They listen to you. And sometimes, they need to be listened to. That's where you come. You listen to them. Even the most intimate secrets are told sometimes. This exchanging of secrets can only be done when you feel safe sharing them with a person. A friend buries your secrets within themselves.

6. Good Memories

Even the most boring party can take a 360 degree turn when you are with your friend. Times like these call for good memories. It would help if you shared loads of good memories. Even when time passes by, a bad day can make an excellent future memory.

Conclusion

It takes a lot of time, care and love to form a strong bond of friendship. We have to give it our best to keep that bond in good condition. Friends are precious to us, and we should make them feel likewise. And with the right person, friendship can last a lifetime.

Chapter 15:
8 Signs That Someone Is Not Your Soulmate

When you find yourself in a relationship, everything feels fantastic. There are confused feelings everywhere, but those confusing feelings are just for the beginning. But we all do wonder if we'll ever find " the one." When we first enter a relationship, you may wonder if this is your soulmate. But sometimes, we want that one person to be our soulmate, but things just aren't meant to be that way. Here are a few signs that someone is not your soulmate.

1. **It is tough to trust them:**

If you feel yourself constantly spying about the whereabouts and motives of your partner because you feel like your partner is not honest with you, then you know that this person is not your soulmate. The reason behind this is that you can't just spend your whole life on the lookout. When you can't trust your soulmate no matter how much you try, you know that your partner is doing some shady stuff. A soulmate will be honest with their relationship even when you are not around because we all know, " Without trust, there is no relationship."

2. **You don't connect at an emotional level:**

In a relationship, you need to know all about your partner, about his life, his work, his future ambitions because if your connection with your partner is just surface level and you don't know anything about them, then you know that is not the "one." A soulmate would want to dig deeper into your soul and would want to know everything about you. Still, if you feel like they are not investing in the relationship and are not working for it, you may think that they are not interested in you or your life like a soulmate should be.

3. Your partner has different values than you:

Everyone has different values and meanings of life, but are these values too much further in your relationship? If so, then you know, this is not your soulmate. Indeed, a relationship requires compromise, but nobody can sacrifice too much, and having different values may as well result in that. Soulmates would have an essential, shared vision for the future.

4. He doesn't enhance your life:

A soulmate is someone who shows you a better side of yourself and life. A soulmate will make you feel complete, make you feel happy when you feel low, and give you the confidence you need. But if your partner makes no effort to help your personal growth or at least make you feel happy in your hard times, then you know that that is not your soulmate.

5. You wish to explore other interests:

It is entirely normal for a person that is in a relationship to find someone else attractive; after all, we all are human beings, but if you start picturing yourself with someone else and start wishing that you were single so you could explore other interests, then that is a huge sign you need to consider. When you find your soulmate, you would not wish to be single, and although other people still seem attractive, you would not want to leave your partner for them.

6. Your partner judges you:

All human beings have different views on life. Everybody thinks differently; indeed, there are things you and your partner do not have legal opinions on, and that is completely fine unless your partner starts judging you for doing something they don't like. Yes, a relationship does need compromise, but that surely does not mean that your partner gets the right to judge you because you did not compromise and still did something they don't like. A soulmate would never consider you for anything you do; a soulmate will understand you in the best possible way.

7. You don't feel the urge to text back:

Everybody knows that when you like someone, you reply to their messages as soon as you can. It is like a human being not to seem rude to the people they like, but if you don't want to reply to your partner, are you sure they are "the one"? If every other text you receive bothers you, and you don't feel that interested in them, you know that this person is not the one you were looking for.

8. **You don't just feel like telling him something important you:**

When you find the one, you want to tell them everything about yourself, including the essential things. But do you feel that way about your partner like you want to say everything about every day, or you just don't bother to tell? If you don't, then you know that he is not the one.

Conclusion:

Don't feel disheartened if you haven't found the right one yet because someone is made especially for you, and one day you will find your soulmate.

Chapter 16:
6 Tips To Find The One

Finding someone who matches our criteria can be a difficult task. We always look for a person who is a knight in shining armor. And by time, we make our type. We are finding someone who looks and behaves like our ideal one. We always fantasize about our right one. No matter how hard it may seem to find someone, we should never lose hope. Sharing is always beneficial. And if you trust someone enough to share your life with them, then it's worth the risk to be taken. The person you chose depends upon you only. The advice can only give you an idea, and you have to act on your own.

Now, when looking for someone from scratch can be difficult for many of us. That person can either be the wrong one or the right one. Only time can tell you that. But you both need to grow together to know if you can survive together. And if not, then separation is the only possible way. But if you find the right one, then it will all be good. You have to have faith in yourself. Be your wingman and go after whatever you desire.

1. Be Patient

When looking for someone you want to spend your time with, someone you want to dedicate a part of your life to, you have to devote your time looking for the one. Be patient with everyone you meet so you will get to know them better. They will be more open towards you when you give them time to open. Doing everything fast will leave you confused. Don't only talk with them. Notice their habits, share secrets and trust them. They will be more comfortable around you when they think that you are willing to cooperate.

2. Keep Your Expectations Neutral

When you find someone for you, they can either leave you disappointed or satisfied. That all depends on your expectations. If you wait for prince charming and get a knight, then you will be nothing but uncomfortable with them. Keep them neutral. Try to make sure that you get to know a person before passing your judgment.

3. Introduce Them To Your Friends

The people who love you tend to get along together. The first thing we do after finding a competitor is telling a friend. We usually go for the people our loved one has chosen for us. While finding the one is all you. They can play a part in giving advice, but they can't decide for you. When we see one, we want everyone to get to know them.

4. Don't Be Discouraged

You are 30 and still haven't found anyone worth your time. If so, then don't get discouraged. That love comes to us when we least expect it. You have to keep looking for that one person who will brighten your days and keep you happy. Please don't go looking for it. It will come to you itself and will make you happy.

5. Look Around You

Sometimes our journey of finding the one can be cut short when we see the one by our side—someone who has been our friend or someone who was with us all along. You will feel happier and more comfortable with finding the right person within your friend. It will make things much more manageable. And one day, you will realize that he was the one all this time. Sometimes we can find one in mutual friends. They may be strangers, but you know a little about them already. However, finding the one within your friend can save you a lot of trouble.

6. Keep The Sparks Fresh

Whatever happens, don't let your spark die because it will become the source of your compassion. It will make a path for you to walk on with your ideal one. Keep that passion, that love alive. If there is no spark, then you will live a life without any light. So, make your partner and yourself feel that compassion in your growth.

Conclusion

Finding one can be a difficult job, but once we find them, they can make us the happiest in the world. And if that person is honest with you, then there is nothing more you should need in one. You can always change your partner until you find the one because they are always their ones too. You have to focus on finding your own.

Chapter 17:

10 Thoughts That Can Destroy Relationships

You might enjoy the beauty and joy that comes with being in a loving and committed relationship, but it's not always butterflies and beds of roses. It's ubiquitous for you or your partner to transform your insecurities into fears and negative thoughts, but they don't treat you right; they may take a toll on your relationship. Negative thoughts may turn into negative actions, which can lead to unhealthy communication, and could impact how you start seeing your significant other. If you relate to any of the below thoughts, it might be time to reevaluate your relationship and how you view the situation.

1. They don't love me anymore:

Although it's pretty common to worry about whether the sparks of love are still alive in your partner's heart or not, constantly asking them whether they still love you might do more harm than good. It could stir up a lot of conflicts based on your insecurities and fears. Even if your partner reassures you by saying that they love you, it could put them in doubt as to there must be a matter causing these concerns. Instead of swinging and jumping to conclusions, communicate effectively with your partner in a way that's suitable for both of you.

2. The power word "should":

It is more or less a major red flag to not tell your partner about what you're thinking rather than automatically assuming that they should know how to read your mind.

Blaming your partner for understanding the things that are affecting you secretly, like, "he should know how much it bothers me when he doesn't give me time" or "she should understand how busy i am these days" isn't fair at all. You should be able to voice all your frustrations but in a way that you make your partner understand and not push them away.

3. The blame game:

It's easier to point fingers at your partner and blame them for your spoiled mood rather than taking actions against yourself. Blaming them only postpones any improvements that are needed in your relationship. Instead, try talking to them about it. Tell them when they are wrong and apologize for something that you did to hurt them. We can never predict or control others' emotions, but we can very well hold our own.

4. Overactive imagination:

This mostly happens when you're overthinking about a situation and jump straight to conclusions without having any actual evidence. For instance, if your partner is coming home late at night and they're telling you it's because of the heavy workload, you automatically assume it's because they're having an affair and they're lying to you. These may happen when you have a piece of unattended emotional baggage from previous relationships. It's important to understand that you know your partner well, and they will never do such a thing to hurt you. Have a conversation with your partner about this and seek reassurance if needed.

5. Comparing and contrasting:

You start to put your partner under the pressure of unrealistic expectations when you compare them with a person you see as ideal. For example, if you met your best friend's boyfriend and witnessed an action they did, and you wished that your boyfriend should do the same, you might be disrespecting your partner by asking them to change into who they aren't. It's unhealthy to put that sort of pressure on them. Instead, ask your partner politely if they're willing to do that for you since you liked a particular quality or trait in a person, but you should also tell them that they are lovable regardless.

6. Fantasizing:

Unless you are in a toxic relationship, reminiscing and fantasizing about someone other than your partner might badly affect your relationship. It's because you will keep thinking about the possibilities of being with someone else rather than working on the flaws of your relationship. This might destroy your relationship in ways you can't even imagine.

7. All or nothing:

Seeing your partner as a perfect human being without mistakes, flaws, or imperfections is an idea for destruction. Having extreme thoughts that they can do no wrong or thinking that they always do the wrong thing can mess up with your own and your partner's mental health. Try accepting their failures and mistakes, and keep in mind that, like you, they're just ordinary human beings.

8. Label slinging:

Constantly putting labels on your partner, like calling them lazy when they couldn't complete their chores or calling them insensitive if they don't address a particular issue, may cause problems in your relationship. Instead, we should try to see the positive things in them and help them improve themselves.

9. You think you can't compete with their ex:

Their ex is their ex for a reason. Constantly trying to be like them and asking about them isn't helpful in any way; it can make your relationship weak and your partner frustrated.

10. You think that you're hard to love:

Worrying about pushing your partner away while addressing your insecurities is normal, but that doesn't in any way mean that you're hard to love. Everyone is special and unique in their tracks and can be loved by their partner no matter what.

Conclusion:

While these thoughts might be the perfect recipe to destroy your relationship, a little effort, and hard work into it can go a long way and save your relationship.

Chapter 18:
6 Behaviours That Keep You Single

Dating may not be as easy as it is shown in all those romantic Hollywood movies. There is so much more than appearance and stability in dating someone. And when you are old enough to be involved with someone, you sometimes find yourself uninterested. You think about how everyone your age has already started dating while you are back there eating junk and watching Netflix. It might appear to you that being in a relationship is tiresome, and you stop trying for it. Everyone has a different preference when it comes to finding someone for themselves. You tend to look for someone that matches your knight in the shining armor, which makes it hard for you to find someone you need.

Be true to you yourself while finding someone to date. Looking for someone with the expectation that you are rich and handsome would be foolish. It would be best if you worked on yourself more than that. Make yourself ease around with people but no so much that they start to get annoyed. Don't get in your way.

1. **Trust Is Essential**

Trusting each other is an important factor for dating someone. If you don't trust your partner even in the slightest, then nothing will matter. You will constantly doubt each other. Both of you will eventually fall apart if there is no trust. And if you have trust issues, it will be difficult for you to find someone worthy. But, if you trust too quickly, then it's only natural that you will break your bubble of expectations. Be friendly. Try to get to know them properly before making any assumptions about them. You don't want to go around hesitating about everything. Find yourself a reliable partner that trusts you too.

2. **Too Many Expectations**

Expecting too much from your partner will lead to only one thing. It leads towards Disappointment. It would help if you let them be. Don't expect things to go your way always. Your knight in the shining armor may be a bookworm because people find love in the most unexpected places. It doesn't always mean to keep no expectations at all. To keep the expectations low. You will get surprised constantly when you don't know what's coming your way. Don't let people cloud your judgment, and keep high standards about a relationship. Everyone has their share of ups and downs. Comparison with others will not be suitable for your relationship.

3. **Have Self-Confidence**

One has to respect itself before anything else can. You have to have self-esteem in you for people to take you seriously. It is true "you can't love someone unless you learn to love yourself first." You tend to feel insecure about yourself. Everything around you seems too perfect for you. And you constantly think that your partner will stop loving you one day. That fear of yours will get you nowhere. Try to give yourself as much care you can. It doesn't hurt to be loved.

4. **Don't Overthink**

You found a guy, and He seems to be excellent. But you start to overthink it. Eventually, you let go. That is what you shouldn't have done. Just try to go with the flow sometimes. Don't try too hard for it. Go for it the easy way. Overthinking will lead you to make up scenarios that never happened. Just let it be and see where it goes. Be easy so people can approach you. Think, don't overthink.

5. **Involving Too Many People**

When you initially start dating, you get nervous. People get help from their friends sometimes. But it is not necessary to get every move through them. Involving them in everything will only get your partner get uncomfortable and get you frustrated. People tend to give a lot of opinions of their own. You will get confused. So, it is good to keep these things to yourself. Be mindful in giving them a brief report from time to time. However, keep them at a reasonable distance.

6. **Giving Up Too Quickly**

If it doesn't work initially, it does not mean that it will never work. Patience is an essential element when it comes to dating anyone. Don't give up too quickly. Try to make it work until it's clear that it won't. Give it your all. Compromise on things you can. Because if both of you are not willing to compromise, it will not work between you both. It will work out in the end if it's meant to be. Don't push it if it's not working too.

Conclusion

It is hard; it keeps going at a pace. But all you must need is that spark that keeps it alive. Make it work until it doesn't. Go for it all. Make commitments only when you are sure about your choice. And be true to your words. Who wants to be single forever?

Chapter 19:

Ten Signs Your Crush Likes You

The weak knees you get when you see them, the fantastic smell of their cologne that you can't get enough of, the skipping of your heartbeat when you see their smile or hear their laughter, your face lighting up when you see their pictures. Yeah yeah, we know that feeling very well; YOU'VE GOT A CRUSH! It happens to almost all of us. Maybe there's a co-worker who caught your eye or a classmate that you exchange glances. Or perhaps it could be a total stranger that you have just met and pretty soon started liking them.

You keep thinking about them and their dreamy eyes, their pleasant bright smile, their oh so perfectly structured face, and their lips that are so... but wait! Aren't we getting too much ahead of ourselves?

Maybe, just maybe, they've shown some signs too. They say a crush is called so because they leave you feeling crushed if they don't reciprocate your feelings. But if you've wished upon your lucky star and maybe this time, your star took pity on you and have answered your prayer, then your case might become different than the one I just mentioned.

Getting suffocating and thought-provoking mixed signals from your crush might drive you crazy. You are always left wondering, hoping if the indicative signs mean anything. That may be your crush likes you back too. If you are plucking the poor petals of your hundredth rose and enchanting, 'He loves me/He loves me not,' then save it for later, pretty please?

We are here for you, and using our expertise, we will help you figure out if you are your crush's crush too.

Here are ten signs (in no particular order) that will help you analyze if your crush likes you back:

1. **Their eyes are fixated on you:**

They say that the eyes are windows to the soul. A study has found out that people unconsciously fixate their eyes on the things they want the most. People tend to keep eye contact with someone they like, apart from the few shy ones who might not like its intensity; perhaps when you will catch them looking at you, they will look away and blush. But shy or not, you have to notice their pupils. Studies show that an individual's pupil dilates when they see someone they like. They also tend to blink more often while watching their crush. If you feel like you are being stared at by your crush or catches them stealing glances at you, and they smile afterward, then consider yourself lucky. And if he's directly locking eyes while talking to you, then that's just the cherry on top of your sundae!

2. **Notice their body language:**

It is said that actions speak louder than words. Have you ever noticed how you feel around them? Do you get nervous, hyper, shy, or suddenly quiet? Or most importantly, if your crush feels the exact same emotions around you. If he gets flustered or fidgets a little more than usual, or starts to blush or sweat while talking to you, then maybe it's a sign he likes you back. You should also notice that when your crush is standing with you, his feet must be pointing towards you. Weird right? But hey, I don't make the rules. When we are interested in someone, our body naturally leans towards them to be closer. This is a subconscious action that signifies interest. So, the next time you're having a conversation with your crush, notice if he leans in and sits forward with his arms uncrossed, having constant eye contact and listening to you attentively.

3. **They're not afraid to open up to you:**

It's normal to develop trust issues considering we suffer from terrible experiences, like heartbreaks and betrayals, in our lives. We might have built a protective wall around ourselves to keep people from hurting us. But when we are around someone we trust, those walls come crumbling down without us even realizing it. Whether it's about them spending their next vacations abroad, or their future college plans, or maybe their deepest darkest secrets, they don't hesitate to talk about all of it to you. Experts say, vulnerability nurtures attraction and develops a sense of trust by fostering deeper feelings of closeness. So, if your crush is vulnerable and weak around you and does not shy pouring out their heart to you, then you must be someone really special to them.

4. **They want to know a lot more about you:**

From your favorite color to your favorite food, to your favorite book, and even your grandma's birthday! They want to know every single detail about you. They remember the important dates and details of your life, even those that subconsciously slipped out from your tongue. Not only this, they never get tired from hearing about you and asking all about you. They might even watch your favorite tv show or read your favorite book to impress you. They make small gestures from the particulars that you have told them. And they are always looking for more opportunities to get to know you better.

5. Always willing to help you:

Men thrive on solving women's problems. I guess it's something biological that men always feel the need to provide for the women he cares about, and vice versa. Whether it's giving her his jacket in the cold or her bringing him warm soup when he's feeling down, it all comes down to how much the individual cares about the other person. Your crush eagerly offers you help with just anything and is always available to lend you a hand whenever you need it. The term 'hero instinct' has been given to men who are always ready to help the women of their liking.

6. They preen themselves around you:

As soon as you enter the room, you see them adjust their clothes, sleek back their hair, or touch their face, then know that they are trying to look presentable and impressive in front of you. Preening around the people we like is a subconscious way to advertise our romantic interest. We tend to want to look the best around them. From wearing our best outfits to smelling fresh and pleasant and making efforts to make oneself look attractive.

7. They become flirty/playful around you:

Another thing to notice is that if your crush is being flirtatious or funny around you. They might try to get your attention and show affection by being playful in a light-hearted and silly way. They might even call you funny nicknames, tease you, or joke around you. It might also be a sarcastic comment or a light punch on the arm or simply laughing with you on random stuff.

8. Their friends act weird when you're around:

If your crush's friends start acting weird when they see you, the chances are that your crush has already told them about you (which, by the way, is basically guaranteed. I mean, who does not say to their friends about their love interest?). Anyways, look for the signs as to how their friends act when you are near them. Do they say their name out loud? Do they giggle or whisper to each other? Do they give you two a playful smile and leave you two alone? Do they randomly start to tell you great things about your crush? Or maybe, they might even ask point-blank if you like the person!

As for you, play along, and maybe their friends would get some sense into them, and they will finally as you out.

9. They try to be always near you:

Do you ever go to a party, hang out with your group of friends, or go to any gathering for that matter but always end up beside your crush? Or perhaps they're making excuses and efforts to see you more often, like a mistaking call or text that results in them asking you out. This might be another sign that your crush likes you; that is, they are trying to get into your proximity. They will try and make sure to spend as much time as they can with you. Whether it's about trying that new restaurant or studying for the English test together, you will see them hovering around you quite often.

10. Their mood changes when you hang out with someone else:

Suppose you are engaged in a deep, meaningful conversation, walking side by side, or just simply laughing with someone from the opposite sex, and you catch your crush feeling gloomy and staring intensely at you both, or walking out of the room, or even joining you guys. In that case, chances are they might be feeling protective or jealous. They want to get all your attention and not share you with anyone else, which is highly adorable. But beware! There is a difference between being playfully jealous and being full-on psychotic possessiveness, which is a huge red flag, and you should probably then stay away from them.

In the end, it is advisable not to assume anything based on just signs and to gut up and tell them how you feel about them. If they reciprocate your feelings, then good for you. If not, then trust me, it'll not be the end of the world; at least you'll be sure of their feelings towards you. And remember, there's always someone out there who would want to be with you. You'll just have to wait and see where destiny will take you.

If you found this video helpful, don't forget to like, subscribe, comment, and share this with someone important to you. I hope you learned something valuable today. Take care, have a good rest, and till the next video ☺

Chapter 20:

7 Signs You Have Found A Keeper

Are you looking for Mr. or Mrs. Right? Or do you think you have found the right person, but how can you be sure? Sometimes, we meet someone who seems like the person you would want to spend your whole life with, but during those times, someone is in for a quick hookup. The only partners worth keeping are the ones that give you the positive vibes that you need after a dull and tedious day, the ones that make you feel happy, and your relationship doesn't feel boring at all. Here are signs that you have found a keeper.

1. They inspire you to become a better person:

When we meet someone very kind, helpful and overall a friendly person that person usually inspires us to be better and luckily the world is full of friendly people. Is your partner like this too? Is he warm, kind, and helpful? Does he inspire you to become a better version of yourself? Then you know you have found yourself a keeper. You know you have found the right person when your partner works hard, gives you and his family time, and has his life organized.

2. **They are always there:**

There are times when we all suffer when things get tough to handle. At times like these, a person always needs support and love to get through the hard times. If your partner is there for you even when you can't defend yourself and they cheer you up, you know that this is a keeper. A perfect partner is someone who knows how to make you laugh even when you are crying, your partner will never believe the things people talk about behind your back, and he would never hesitate to lend you a hand when you need some help.

3. **They know you more than yourself:**

Sometimes it fascinates us how someone can know us more than we know ourselves; it feels perfect when someone knows how or what we are thinking. If your partner knows what you are feeling without telling them, then they are the one. Does your partner know what you are comfortable with? Can they tell when you feel upset? Do they motivate you to do better and ask you to chase after your dreams? If so, then don't waste more time thinking if this is the right person for you because it is.

4. **Your interests are common:**

Sure, opposites attract, but too many differences are not usually suitable for someone's relationship. It would help if you had a common interest with your partner, like having common beliefs, values, and religious perspectives. When you agree on these things, your bond will become more robust, and you would find it very easy to live with that person.

5. They are honest with you:

Finding an honest person is a tiring thing to do; many people lie more than twice a day, but how can that affect your relationship? The right one may lie about small things that don't matter that much, like whether the color suits you or not; they may say those things to make you feel good about yourself, but lying about other things like financial status, health, or fidelity can be more serious. A true keeper would never keep these things from you, and they would always be honest with you even if the truth upsets you.

6. They don't feel tired of you:

Although everyone needs some space, even from the person they love the most, he will never get tired of you if he is the one. Your partner will never feel bored with you; on the contrary, your partner will never get tired of looking at you, admiring you, being with you, and above all, love you. When a person is so in love with you that they want to spend every second of their life with you, then you know you have found a keeper.

7. You are a part of their dreams:

Can your partner not even imagine your life without you? Has your partner already planned his future, and you are a big part of it? If so, you know that this one's a keeper. You both have reached a point in your lives where even thinking about living without each other sounds absurd, and then you know that you have found a keeper.

Conclusion:

A keeper is someone that loves, cherishes, and cares for you like no one has ever had. Don't worry if you haven't found your keeper, and it is just a matter of time before you do because, for every one of us, there is someone out there.

Chapter 21:

7 Reasons Why Men Cheat

Men and women may cheat for different reasons, but it's likely due to the way men and women are socialized rather than any innate differences between them. The more we, as a society, move away from socialization and patriarchy, the less we see those gender differences in cheating behavior. However, nonetheless, research shows that men are more likely to cheat than women. The ratio is 20% of men have admitted to cheating compared to 13% of women.

We should never forget that our minds are more resilient than we give them credit for. Cheating in a relationship is solely that person's fault, no matter the circumstances. It can always be avoided if the person wants to. There are many reasons why men cheat, along with what defines cheating and signs to watch out for. Here are some reasons and behaviors that might apply to people of all genders but could be relevant to men.

1. They're Looking For A Way Out

Sometimes the first step for a man to get out of a relationship is to cheat. Although people of all genders might cheat, for this reason, men are most likely to do it. This is because men are less likely to have difficult conversations with their partners and seldom tell their own needs in a relationship. So, they see cheating as the only way out. Instead of having to bear the difficult conversation with their partner when they're done with their relationship, they escape through it all by the act of cheating and having an affair.

2. They're Looking For A Connection

Cheating doesn't always happen for physical reasons only, despite what gender norms might tell us about men. Feeling unseen, unheard, or disconnected from their partners can also contribute as a factor for it. Men are much less likely to have a sound social support system, and those things can hurt and make them go into a zone where they feel protected. In those instances, if a woman shows compassion and support, they welcome her with open arms. It might start with a friendship with someone who will make him feel better about himself, and hence, an emotional connection forms.

3. They Have Sociopathic or Narcissistic Traits

If a partner has cheated, there could be more than just finding a way out of their relationship. There can be narcissistic tendencies or sociopathic traits involved. They could be someone who doesn't care about their partner's feelings, and they might do it simply because they want to. When an opportunity to cheat presents itself, they go towards it without giving a damn about their partner.

4. Revenge Cheating

Some people act on their impulses and cheat out of anger, jealousy, or desire revenge. It's not necessary that their partner might have cheated on them; even if they have done something slight to upset them (like having a close friendship with another man), they'll end up cheating on their partner to make a point.

5. Struggles With Substance Abuse

Cheating becomes more likely if one is dealing with a substance abuse problem. Substance addiction can create an impulse-driven and more immature version of ourselves. Many relationships tend to fall apart if one of the two partners has become addicted to a substance and acts subconsciously on their impulse.

6. They Seek Validation

If someone is not getting validation in their relationship, then insecurity and low self-esteem can drive them to cheat. If they don't feel attracted enough to their partner, they may cheat to seek external validation. Sexual issues can also cause someone to look for someone newer to prove themselves to.

7. They're Emotionally Immature

Emotional immaturity is sometimes the core of why men cheat. Since childhood, men are expected and taught not to talk about their feelings and emotions. This inability to speak leads to several issues and conflicts in their relationships. By the time you know it, they are having an affair and cheating on their significant other. Cheating can be an essential consequence of poor judgment, lack of willpower, self-control, and immaturity. A mature man will always talk about his feelings and resolve conflicts and issues with his partner.

Conclusion:

Being cheated on can be the worst trauma anyone can experience, and there can be so many reasons it might have happened in different relationships and contexts. But no matter the reason, it cannot be denied that infidelity forces both of you to step back. Analyze what went wrong and decide how you both want to move forward from there.

Chapter 22:
7 Ways To Deal With An Overly Jealous Partner

Being jealous in a relationship seems cute at first, but it can really kill the love you and your partner have for each other after a while. You'll probably start to see the negative aspects of over jealousy pretty clearly. Some people have bad experiences and trust issues due to their past relationships, so being in a relationship with a jealous person shouldn't necessarily be a deal-breaker. It can be started by finding why your partner is feeling the way they feel, especially when you haven't given them a reason to mistrust you in the first place.

If your partner is being aggressive and trying to control what you're doing, you might want to try to work together with them to fix the issue. It will give them the reassurance they need and create a closer bond between you two. If your partner is turning red with jealousy lately, here are some signs for you to deal with them.

1. **Talk About Their Fears and Anxieties**

It would be best to calmly sit your partner down with you and ask them what's going on in their mind if you feel like your partner's jealousy is getting off the hook. Make sure you're listening to them fully attentively, and don't be scared to express how their thoughts affect you. Danielle B. Grossman, a California licensed marriage and family therapist, says, "Do not try to minimize, negate or 'fix' the fears. Do not try to bully your partner's fear into submission. Do not belittle, humiliate, shame, and threaten the fear." Always be empathetic and give them your undivided attention. Make sure you never attack your partner and make them trust that they can confide in you.

2. **Don't Get Defensive About Your Behavior**

If your partner is accusing you of something that is far from true, do not feed the fire by jumping right away into an argument. Evaluate the situation first. If you instantly try to get defensive, your partner will misinterpret your reaction or may get even angrier. Try to be patient first and deal with the situation calmly. Reassure them that whatever they're thinking isn't right, and you're always going to be with them no matter what.

3. **Be Extra Affectionate**

After discussing the reasons for their jealousy, show your partner extra love, during this weak and vulnerable time. This is the time to be more generous with your affection. Try to touch them more, make small gestures for them, and be supportive throughout this time. Of course, this means that you should take the abuse if extremely unhealthy jealousy is present. Don't let them force you into situations that you are uncomfortable dealing with.

4. **Create Boundaries**

Setting boundaries in your relationship isn't a negative thing at all. Loads of people in healthy relationships create a line to understand each other's emotions and priorities better. People should be aware of their selves even within a relationship. According to a Ph.D. psychologist Leslie Becker-Phelps, "You need to know what you like and dislike, what you're comfortable with versus what scares you, and how you want to be treated in the given situations." So, try your best not to let your mental health affect by your partner's conflicts.

5. **Be Available and Responsive:**

Although this issue is something that your partner needs to fix on their own, it can still help the situation get better if you're responsive when they reach out to you. If you're there when your partner needs you the most, and you tend to comfort them, it can help calm their jealous habits. This takes a lot of effort, without a doubt, but if your partner notices that you're available and receptive, then the trust between you two will only grow stronger with time.

6. Revisit The Issue and Be Patient

Over jealousy is an issue that can't be fixed overnight. You must be patient with your partner and show them now and then that you're willing to work on this problem together by supporting and discussing their fears. It can indeed be time-consuming and emotionally draining, but don't let it stop you from trying to work things out with your partner. Take baby steps, celebrate small victories until it isn't an issue anymore.

7. Rebuild Your Trust

If your partner is losing trust in you, make sure you gain it back by doing small things, such as facetiming them and texting them throughout the day, explaining to them why you're running late, or taking a rain check in advance if you know you're busy that day. Reassure them with positive statements, and this will eventually put your partner's fears at ease.

Conclusion

There's no magic spell or easy way to deal with a jealous partner, but if you want to make the relationship work, then put effort into it. Get your partner to trust you, be empathetic with them and talk about their feelings. This little bump in the road can probably go away, which will help you in the long run.

Chapter 23:

5 Signs Someone Only Likes You As A Friend

There's nothing like the feeling of getting friend-zoned by a guy/girl you so desperately wanted to be with. When theoretical physicists started talking about black holes, they were probably referring to the friend zone. You find yourself drooling and crushing hard over them, only to find out that they have never reciprocated those feelings. Spotting the signs that they just want to be friends with you and nothing more is always disappointing. But the sooner you see them, the easier it will be for you to move on.

Sure, it might be a little complex for you at first, as some people tend to be very poor in communicating and can give mixed signals, which might make you confused. It could lead to a bunch of misunderstandings between you two and may also cause you to daydream about them when there isn't anything for you. Here are some subtle signs that they only like you as a friend.

They Never Get Jealous

Overly jealous people can be considered toxic ones, and jealousy isn't always a good thing. But sometimes, in small amounts, it might show that one person does care enough about the other to want them all to themselves. If the person you like never gets jealous when you're flirting with other people, or when others are showing their interest in you, then it means they don't care about your love life and sees you only as a friend who's having fun. On the contrary, if they show some emotion or are affected by you flirting with others, it might mean they're interested in you.

They Are Always Trying To Set You Up With Their Friends
If you're romantically interested in someone, then it's not a great sign if they're your matchmaker all the time. Relationships might start like this only in the movies, while the reality is different. It's improbable that someone would set up a person they like with their friend or their acquaintance. If they're constantly on your nerve asking you to date people or are being your wing person, then it's a sign they consider you only as a friend.

There's No Flirting From Their
If two people are really into each other and spend most of their time together, then it's nearly impossible for them not to flirt, even if it's a little bit. It's always in their subconscious mind to praise and appreciate someone they like. While some people aren't the flirty type, and some are just straight-up awkward or shy, we can always filter out if they're petrified or just downright ignoring us. If they don't flirt with you ever, like in any way, or if your flirty remarks make them uncomfortable and they reject your attempts straight away, then it could mean that they're not interested in you.

They Discuss Their Love Life With You

Most of the time, people wouldn't gush about their romantic lives in front of you if they seem interested in you. It would simply send out the signal that they aren't available to you. They might talk about their ex-lovers to try to make you jealous or talk about people who are into them to try to impress you, but that's an entirely different kettle of fish. While it can be hard to tell the difference, see if he genuinely seeks your love advice or seems overly interested in someone else. That would mean he likes someone else and not you.

They Rarely Text You Or Asks About You

When someone likes you, they tend to find excuses to text you and talk to you all the time. They might start by asking silly questions that they already knew the answer to, or may indulge in deep conversations with you, or direct the subject elsewhere so that they have a chance to talk to you. They might even ask your friends or friends about you and try to find you when you're not around. On the contrary, if they hardly text you or call you or even don't try to communicate with you, then it's a clear sign that they might not be interested in you.

Conclusion

You should try and be clear about your feelings and ask them to do the same since day one, as it could save both of you from confusion and getting mixed signals and fantasizing about something that doesn't even exist in the first place. You cannot make someone love you, no matter how much you wish you could.

Chapter 24:
5 Ways To Reject Someone Nicely

Rejecting someone can be pretty hard as we never want that to happen to us as well. But leading onto something that you don't wish to will end up getting you both frustrated and confused. So, it is better to be true to yourself and the other person who feels something for you. That one-sided feeling has to come to a stop at some point, and only you can stop that. You don't need to blame yourself, but an apology would be an excellent way to reject someone. It is, no doubt, the most challenging part of dating.

Try to inform them as soon as possible, that way you will not be wasting any of their time. It can be uncomfortable and awkward to you and them, but it is necessary to do it. And we need to be as gentle and kind as possible while rejecting someone. It can be as hard as getting rejected yourself. It would be best if you picture yourself in their place. It would help if you treated them the way exactly as you want to be treated while getting rejected by someone.

1. Be Honest To Them
When you are rejecting someone, you need to avoid small talks as much as possible. It will only waste your time as well as yours. Be as honest as

possible for yourself. It would be best if you told them all the valid reasons for their failure. Keep calm the whole time. Try to be straightforward with the person in front of you. There is no point in dragging things out if the income will be the same in the end. Make sure you try not to hurt them and disappoint them. And after all this, you both have your journey to continue.

2. Choose Your Wording Carefully

You both might go your ways after the rejection, but the words you said will stay with them forever. You need to choose your wording very carefully and make sure it sounds right when spoken. The person in front of you deserves an excellent explanation with a few words of encouragement for him to move on from this rejection. Make sure you choose each word respectfully. Appreciate them for confronting you too. Don't sound too sorry for them. And be very clear on what you have to deliver.

3. Do It In Person

The worst rejection you can give anyone is through a message or a phone. Try to go yourself to reject someone. If you are unable to reach the person for talking for any reason, you have to make sure that you keep the conversation on the phone as authentic as possible. Try to go yourself to give them support. Show them that it is hard for you both to sit there. Its common courtesy to make the other person think that this conversation is vital for you. Show up on time and make sure you deliver your message fully.

4. Don't Give False Hope

If you are not interested in someone, a clear, blunt "no" will do. Don't go by the fear of breaking a heart. You will give that person false hope about dating, and you both will end up unhappy about it. It will waste a lot of your time and theirs. They will move on more quickly if you let them go early. You cannot force the feeling into you. And the other person would be thankful too for your honesty which saved you both from something that was never meant to happen. Just let them be and let them recover from you on their own. That will be the best you could do for them.

5. Don't Blame Them

It would help if you accepted the fact that you are going to hurt them no matter what. And the truth is it was never their fault, to begin with. We cannot choose whom we like in our life. When reasoning, give a lot of "I" statements. Don't point out their issues and faults, and it will only make them hurt more. It is always easier to use the "It's not you, it me "approach with the person you are rejecting. They have to bear with the bad news on their own.

Conclusion

We all want that spark in a relationship, and the lack of it can be equally disappointing to you. But if the other person feels that spark, then you have to light it out quickly. They should move on with someone new in their life and you with someone who can give you that same spark you were craving.

Chapter 25:

7 Habits To Change Your Life

Consistently, habit drives you to do what you do—regardless of whether it's a matter of considerations or conduct that happens naturally. Whatever that is, imagine a scenario where you could saddle the power of your habits to improve things. Envision a day to day existence where you have a habit for finishing projects, eating admirably, staying in contact with loved ones, and working to your fullest potential. At the point when you have an establishment of beneficial routines, you're setting yourself up for a full, sound, and effective life.

Here are 7 habits that Can change your entire life.

1. Pinpoint and Focus Entirely on Your K eystone Routine.

Charles Duhigg, in his power book stipulates the essence of recognizing your Keystone Habit—the habit you distinguish as the main thing you can change about your life. To discover what that is for you, ask yourself, what continually worries you? Is it something you would that you like to stop, or something you would do and prefer not to begin? The cornerstone habit is distinctive for everybody, and it might take a couple of meetings of profound thought to pinpoint precisely what that habit is. Whichever propensity you're chipping away at, pick each in turn. More than each in turn will be overpowering and will improve your probability of neglecting to improve any habits. Be that as it may, don't really accept that you can just change one thing about yourself; it's really the inverse. Dealing with this one Keystone Habit can have a positive gradually expanding influence into the remainder of your life also.

2. Recognize Your Present Daily Practice and the Reward You Get From It.

Suppose you need to fabricate a habit for getting to the workplace a half hour early every day. You need to do this since you figured the extra peaceful time in the morning hours will assist you with being more gainful, and that profitability will be compensated by an expanded feeling of occupation fulfilment, and a generally speaking better workplace. As of now, you get to the workplace simply on schedule. Your present routine is to take off from your home in a hurry, at the specific time you've determined that (without traffic or episode) will get you to chip away at time. Your award is investing some additional energy at your home in the first part of the day, spending an additional half hour dozing or "charging your batteries" for the day ahead.

3. Take the Challenges Into Consideration

Challenges are regularly prompts that push you to fall once more into old habits. In the case of having to get to work earlier, your challenges may lie in your rest designs the prior night, or in organizing plans with a partner. These difficulties won't mysteriously vanish so you need to consider them. In any case, don't let the presence of challenges, or stress that new difficulties will come up later on, discourage you from setting up your new propensities. In the event that your difficulties incorporate planning with others, make them a piece of your new daily practice, as I'll clarify later. At this moment, basically recognize what the difficulties or obstructions are.

4. Plan and Identifying Your New Routine

Old habits never vanish; they are basically supplanted with new propensities. In the case of getting to the workplace earlier, the new standard includes going out a half hour sooner. On the off chance that the old habit was remunerated with the possibility that you'll have more energy for the day by remaining in your home longer, the new propensity needs to centre around the possibility that more rest doesn't really mean more energy. All in all, you'll need to address what you think you'll be surrendering by supplanting the old habit.

5. Reinforce a 30 Days Challenge.

By and large, your inability to minister beneficial routines basically comes from not adhering to them. A lot of studies show that habits, when performed day by day, can turn out to be important for your daily schedule in just 21 days. So set a beginning date and dispatch your game plan for a preliminary 30-day time span.

6. Empower Your Energy Through Setbacks.

Here and there, it's not simply self-control that runs out. Now and then you are influenced from your ways by life "hindering" new objectives. In the event that something influences you from your test, the best game-plan is to assess the circumstance and perceive how you can get around, finished, or through that deterrent. Notwithstanding, when another propensity is set up, it really turns into our default setting. Assuming your standard habits are sound, unpleasant occasions are less inclined to lose you from your typical schedules. All in all, we're similarly prone to default to solid habits as we are to self-undermining habits, if those sound habits have become a piece of our ordinary daily practice.

7. Account Yourself and for Your Actions Publicly (Hold Yourself Accountable).

Your encouraging people are the most significant asset you will have at any point. Regardless of whether it's your closest companion, your accomplice or your Facebook posts, being responsible to somebody other than yourself will help you adhere to your objective. Simply remember that "responsible" isn't equivalent to "declaration". Anybody can advise the world they will rise ahead of schedule from here on out. However, on the off chance that that individual has a group of allies behind them, whom they routinely update, they are bound to stay with their new propensity during times when they are building up their new habit and inspiration is coming up short.

www.ingramcontent.com/pod-product-compliance
Lightning Source LLC
LaVergne TN
LVHW010359070526
838199LV00065B/5859